I0019469

Social Media Monetization Mastery

A Complete Course to Turn Your Platforms into Profit

A Complete Step-by-Step Course to Make Money on Facebook, Twitter, YouTube, TikTok & Instagram

By Jordan Blaze

Copyright © 2025 Jordan Blaze

Disclaimer:

This book is for educational and informational purposes only. The strategies and examples shared are based on the author's experience and current platform policies at the time of writing. Results may vary based on individual effort, consistency, and algorithm changes. The author is not responsible for any outcomes resulting from the application of this material.

Table of Contents

Introduction

Why Social Media is the New Goldmine

Who This Book is For

How to Use This Book as a Monetization Course

Module 1: The Monetization Mindset

Lesson 1: Shifting from Consumer to Creator

Lesson 2: Identifying Your Niche and Audience

Lesson 3: Building a Magnetic Personal Brand

Module 2: Facebook Monetization

Lesson 1: Facebook Page vs. Profile – What You Need

Lesson 2: Facebook In-Stream Ads

Lesson 3: Stars, Subscriptions, and Fan Support

Lesson 4: Monetizing with Facebook Groups & Marketplace

Module 3: Twitter (X) Monetization

Lesson 1: Building Authority on Twitter

Lesson 2: Twitter Blue & Ad Revenue Sharing

Lesson 3: Affiliate Marketing & Product Promotion

Lesson 4: Using Threads to Drive Sales

Module 4: YouTube Monetization

Lesson 1: YouTube Partner Program (YPP) Basics

Lesson 2: Earning from Ads, Super Chats & Memberships

Lesson 3: Sponsorships & Brand Collaborations

Lesson 4: Creating Viral and Evergreen Content

Module 5: TikTok Monetization

Lesson 1: Creator Fund vs. Creativity Program

Lesson 2: Going Live, Gifts, and Brand Deals

Lesson 3: Using Affiliate Links Effectively

Lesson 4: Driving Followers to Sales Funnels

Module 6: Instagram Monetization

Lesson 1: Business vs. Creator Accounts

Lesson 2: Sponsored Posts & Story Ads

Lesson 3: Reels Bonus & Affiliate Tools

Lesson 4: Leveraging Bio Links & Product Pages

Module 7: Monetization Tools & Platforms

Must-Have Tools: Linktree, Gumroad, Ko-fi, Canva, ConvertKit

Creating and Selling Digital Products

Using Email Lists for Passive Income

Module 8: Scaling and Automation

Repurposing Content Across Platforms

Scheduling & Automating Like a Pro

When to Outsource & Build a Team

Module 9: Mistakes That Kill Monetization

Platform Violations & Shadowbans

Inconsistent Branding & Content Confusion

Fake Followers, Bots, and Engagement Tricks

Module 10: 30-Day Monetization Action Plan

Week 1: Setup & Strategy

Week 2: Content & Engagement

Week 3: Monetize & Promote

Week 4: Evaluate & Scale

Final Thoughts

Building a Long-Term Digital Empire

Stay Consistent, Stay Authentic

The Journey from Zero to Earning Never Ends

Introduction

Why Social Media is the New Goldmine

We're living in the most powerful era for creators, influencers, and digital hustlers. The same platforms people scroll through for fun—Facebook, Twitter, YouTube, TikTok, and Instagram—are now the most accessible income streams in the world.

No boss. No degree required. Just a phone, Wi-Fi, and a smart content strategy.

If you've ever looked at creators getting paid and thought, "I could do that..."—you're absolutely right. This book is your blueprint. A course-in-a-book. A step-by-step playbook to help you turn posts into profit, attention into income, and followers into fans who support what you do.

Who This Book is For?

Aspiring influencers who want to monetize their platform

Small business owners or freelancers who want to grow sales via social media

Content creators ready to turn engagement into income

Students, 9–5ers, or side hustlers with limited time but big goals

No matter your niche—fashion, sports, tech, education, motivation, or memes—there's a monetization path for you.

How to Use This Book

This isn't just something you read and forget. This is a course in disguise.

Each chapter acts like a module. You'll learn the strategies, then get real-world tips you can apply immediately. Whether you're building from scratch or leveling up your existing audience, you'll find clear, actionable steps.

By the end of this book, you'll understand:

How each major platform pays creators

What types of content drive real money

How to create digital products, get brand deals, and build an online empire

So, turn the page, grab a notebook if you need one, and let's dive into the world of social media monetization.

Your platform is a business. Let's make it profitable.

— Jordan Blaze

Module 1: The Monetization Mindset

Lesson 1: Shifting from Consumer to Creator

Every day, millions of people scroll through social media—liking, commenting, and consuming content. But there's a massive difference between those who consume and those who create.

Consumers spend time. Creators build assets.

If you want to make money on social media, the first shift isn't in your content—it's in your mindset.

Stop scrolling mindlessly. Start studying what works.

Stop comparing your journey to others. Start building your own lane.

You don't need to be famous. You need to be valuable.

Lesson 2: Identifying Your Niche and Audience

Before you monetize, you need clarity:

What do you stand for? Who are you helping? What value do you bring?

Ask yourself:

What topics do I love talking about?

What skills, experiences, or passions can I share?

What problems can I solve for others?

Popular niches that monetize well include:

Personal finance & investing

Fitness & health

Tech & gadgets

Motivation & self-growth

Beauty & fashion

Education & tutorials

Gaming & entertainment

Your goal: become the go-to person for a specific type of content.

Lesson 3: Building a Magnetic Personal Brand

In a noisy online world, a strong personal brand sets you apart.

It's not about logos or fancy editing—it's about clarity, consistency, and connection.

Your personal brand should answer three things:

1. Who you are

2. What you do

3. Why people should follow you

Use a clear profile picture, a short bio that speaks to your value, and a content style that people instantly recognize.

Example:

"Helping young hustlers grow online income with real strategies. No fluff—just facts."

Monetization Mindset Recap:

Shift from being a passive consumer to a focused creator

Find your niche and understand your audience

Build a brand that people trust and follow

Be consistent—growth takes time, but money follows momentum

Next Up: Module 2 – Facebook Monetization

Ready to turn your Facebook presence into income? Let's go.

Module 2: Facebook Monetization

Lesson 1: Facebook Page vs. Profile – What You Need

When it comes to making money on Facebook, using the right setup matters. Many creators make the mistake of trying to monetize a personal profile, but to access Facebook's full suite of monetization tools, you need a Facebook Page.

Why a Facebook Page?

Access to In-Stream Ads, Stars, Subscriptions, and Professional Dashboard

Ability to run Facebook Ads and boost posts

Built-in analytics to track your content performance

Eligible for partner monetization tools if you meet their criteria

Pro Tip: Convert your personal profile into a professional mode to unlock early monetization features even before creating a Page.

Lesson 2: Facebook In-Stream Ads

Facebook pays creators through In-Stream Ads that play before, during, or after your video.

Requirements to qualify:

10,000 Page followers

600,000 total minutes viewed in the last 60 days

At least 5 active video uploads

Must comply with Monetization Policies

How much can you earn?

Depending on your niche and audience location, creators earn $1–$10 per 1,000 views.

Success Tip: Create videos that are at least 3 minutes long—this unlocks more ad placements and better payouts.

Lesson 3: Stars, Subscriptions, and Fan Support

Facebook also allows fans to financially support creators.

Stars:

Viewers buy stars and send them during your live videos or video premieres.

Each star = $0.01, and it adds up fast if your audience is loyal.

Subscriptions:

Offer fans monthly memberships with perks (behind-the-scenes content, exclusive lives, etc.). You earn recurring revenue while deepening your community connection.

Eligibility:

10,000 followers OR 250 returning viewers

50,000 post engagements in the last 60 days

180,000 watch minutes over the last 60 days

Real Strategy: Host weekly live sessions where you engage, educate, or entertain—then promote Stars or Subscriptions during the stream.

Lesson 4: Monetizing with Facebook Groups & Marketplace

Beyond official tools, there are smart indirect monetization strategies on Facebook:

1. Facebook Groups:

Build a niche group around your content or brand

Share value-driven content (tips, resources, challenges)

Promote your digital products, services, or affiliate links

Use your group as a funnel to sell courses, ebooks, or consulting

2. Facebook Marketplace:

Ideal for selling digital downloads or merch

Use product listings to drive traffic to your other platforms

Combine with automated messaging to upsell your services

Quick Recap:

Create a Facebook Page to unlock monetization tools

Focus on In-Stream Ads with 3+ minute videos

Encourage fans to support you with Stars and Subscriptions

Use Groups and Marketplace to promote products and build a community

Module 3: Twitter (X) Monetization

Lesson 1: Building Authority on Twitter

To monetize your Twitter (X) account, you first need a strong and engaged presence. This is not about random tweets; it's about establishing authority in your niche.

How to Build Authority:

Be Consistent: Post regularly with value-driven content. Whether it's tips, threads, opinions, or updates—make sure you're providing something people can't ignore.

Engage with Your Audience: Reply to comments, retweet insightful content, and start conversations. Build relationships with your followers.

Leverage Hashtags: Use trending and niche-specific hashtags to increase your visibility.

Pro Tip: Create Twitter threads that dive deep into a subject. Threads can go viral, giving you much-needed exposure.

Lesson 2: Twitter Blue & Ad Revenue Sharing

Twitter Blue is a paid subscription service that unlocks various features, and it's becoming an essential tool for monetization.

How Twitter Blue Helps You Monetize:

Verified Badge: Having a verification badge adds credibility and makes your account more attractive to potential sponsors.

Ad Revenue Sharing: If you have Twitter Blue, you can start earning a share of ad revenue from the ads displayed on your tweets.

Longer Tweets & Video Content: With Twitter Blue, you can post longer tweets and videos, allowing for better engagement and monetization.

How to Qualify for Ad Revenue Sharing:

Be a Twitter Blue subscriber.

Create high-quality content that attracts engagement.

Keep a consistent follower base, engaging with both your content and ads.

Success Tip: The more your content resonates with your audience, the more you can earn from ad revenue sharing. Always focus on creating content your followers can relate to.

Lesson 3: Affiliate Marketing & Product Promotion

Twitter is an excellent platform for affiliate marketing, where you promote other people's products and earn a commission for sales made through your referral links.

How to Use Twitter for Affiliate Marketing:

Share Affiliate Links: Post about products or services you believe in. Make sure to include a clear call-to-action and an engaging reason why your followers should consider the product.

Use Pin Tweets: Pin a tweet promoting an affiliate offer to keep it visible on your profile.

Engage & Nurture Your Followers: Build trust with your followers by consistently providing value, so when you do share affiliate links, they're more likely to convert.

Pro Tip: If you have a website or blog, integrate your Twitter affiliate offers with your blog posts or landing pages for higher conversion rates.

Lesson 4: Using Threads to Drive Sales

Twitter threads aren't just for education—they can also drive sales. If you're promoting your products, services, or affiliate offers, use threads to share a story or step-by-step guide that ends with a sales pitch.

How to Use Threads for Sales:

1. Start with a Hook: Grab attention right from the first tweet.

2. Provide Value: Share tips, insights, or personal stories that lead up to your product or service.

3. End with a Clear CTA: Direct your audience to your website, product page, or affiliate link. Don't forget to offer an incentive like a discount or free trial.

Real Strategy: Share success stories in your threads. Talk about how your followers (or customers) benefitted from your services or product, creating social proof.

Quick Recap:

Build authority by consistently posting valuable content and engaging with your audience.

Monetize through Twitter Blue by unlocking revenue sharing and using advanced features.

Use affiliate marketing by promoting products or services and linking to them in your tweets.

Drive sales through Twitter threads by providing value and ending with a strong call-to-action.

Next: Module 4 – YouTube Monetization

Ready to dive into YouTube? Let's explore the essentials of monetizing on the platform.

Module 4: YouTube Monetization

Lesson 1: YouTube Partner Program (YPP) Basics

To make money on YouTube, you need to become a part of the YouTube Partner Program (YPP). This program allows creators to monetize their content through ads, memberships, super chats, and more.

Eligibility for YouTube Partner Program:

1,000 subscribers

4,000 watch hours in the last 12 months

Comply with YouTube's monetization policies

Have a linked AdSense account

Turn on 2-step verification on your Google account

Once you qualify, you can start earning money from the YouTube Partner Program through ads on your videos.

Pro Tip: The quicker you hit your 1,000 subscribers and 4,000 watch hours, the faster you'll start earning revenue. Keep pushing out high-quality, engaging content.

Lesson 2: Earning from Ads, Super Chats & Memberships

Once you're accepted into the YouTube Partner Program, you unlock various ways to earn.

1. Ad Revenue

You'll earn money when ads are displayed on your videos.

YouTube ads come in multiple formats: Display ads, Overlay ads, Skippable video ads, and Non-skippable video ads.

Your earnings depend on the CPM (Cost Per Thousand Impressions), which varies based on audience location, niche, and season.

2. Super Chats and Super Stickers

Super Chats allow viewers to pay to highlight their comments during live streams.

Super Stickers are paid graphics that viewers send during live streams to show support.

You earn money directly from your audience's engagement in live sessions.

3. Channel Memberships

Channel Memberships allow your subscribers to pay a monthly fee in exchange for exclusive perks like badges, emojis, and access to members-only content.

To be eligible for Channel Memberships, you need 30,000 subscribers or more.

Success Tip: Combine Super Chats, live streams, and Channel Memberships to increase your earnings.

Lesson 3: Sponsorships & Brand Collaborations

Another lucrative revenue stream on YouTube is sponsorships. Brands are willing to pay you to promote their products if you have a substantial audience and influence in your niche.

How to Get Sponsorships:

1. Build a Strong, Engaged Community: Brands want to work with creators who have an active, engaged audience.

2. Reach Out to Brands: Don't wait for them to find you—take the initiative by reaching out directly.

3. Join Influencer Platforms: Platforms like Grapevine, Channel Pages, or Famebit connect creators with brands looking for influencers to partner with.

Pro Tip: Make sure your sponsorships feel authentic. Your audience can tell when you're promoting something just for the paycheck, and it can hurt your credibility.

Lesson 4: Creating Viral and Evergreen Content

While monetizing on YouTube, creating viral content (videos that get huge views in a short time) and evergreen content (videos that continue to get views over time) is key to building long-term revenue.

1. Viral Content:

Trend-jacking: Hop on trending topics and viral challenges to get your video in front of a broader audience.

Catchy Titles & Thumbnails: Your title and thumbnail must spark curiosity to encourage viewers to click on your video.

Engagement: Encourage likes, comments, and shares. The more engagement, the more likely YouTube will recommend your video.

2. Evergreen Content:

Educational Videos: Create "how-to" or tutorial videos that continue to provide value long after they are published.

FAQs: Answer common questions in your niche. These types of videos are often searched over time.

Product Reviews: Review products that remain relevant for long periods. These videos continue to bring in new viewers.

Pro Tip: Mix both viral and evergreen content into your strategy. Viral content can give you a quick boost, while evergreen content provides steady growth.

Quick Recap:

Become a part of the YouTube Partner Program to monetize your videos through ads, super chats, and memberships.

Diversify your income by incorporating sponsorships and brand collaborations into your strategy.

Focus on creating both viral and evergreen content to ensure both short-term and long-term monetization.

Next: Module 5 – TikTok Monetization

Now that we've covered YouTube, let's dive into the rapidly growing world of TikTok.

Module 5: TikTok Monetization

Lesson 1: Creator Fund vs. Creativity Program

Practical Step 1: Join the Creator Fund

Eligibility Check: Ensure you have 10,000 followers and 100,000 video views in the last 30 days. If you don't meet this, focus on increasing your engagement by posting consistently and using trending sounds and hashtags.

How to Apply:

1. Open your TikTok app and go to your Profile.

2. Tap the three dots in the top right to open Settings.

3. Scroll to Creator Tools and tap TikTok Creator Fund.

4. Apply by following the instructions, and you'll get access to payments based on views.

Practical Step 2: Maximize Earnings from the Creator Fund

Post Consistently: Post at least 3-5 times a week. Focus on what's trending but always align it with your niche. For instance, if you're in fitness, use trending audio while demonstrating a quick workout.

Engagement is Key: Respond to comments, create duets or stitch videos, and use popular challenges to boost engagement. Higher engagement increases your views and thus your earnings.

Lesson 2: Going Live, Gifts, and Brand Deals

Practical Step 1: Go Live and Start Earning Gifts

Eligibility: You need 1,000 followers to go live.

How to Go Live:

1. Tap the + button on your profile page.

2. Select the Live option from the menu.

3. Write an engaging title, like "Let's talk fitness tips!" or "Q&A session – ask me anything!".

4. Start streaming and interact with your viewers. Ask questions to keep them engaged and encourage them to send virtual gifts.

Practical Step 2: Convert Gifts into Cash

Maximize Live Engagement: Engage with your audience by offering value. Share insights, tell stories, or host contests where the winner gets a shoutout or a free consultation.

How to Redeem Gifts:

1. After your live session, tap your profile and go to Creator Tools.

2. Tap Balance, and you'll see your diamonds (the value of gifts).

3. Convert diamonds to real money and withdraw them.

Practical Step 3: Brand Deals

How to Get Started: If you have a solid following (5,000+), start reaching out to brands.

1. Send direct messages to companies you like and pitch how you can feature their product in a fun, creative TikTok video.

2. Use platforms like Influencity, Upfluence, or TikTok Creator Marketplace to connect with brands looking for influencers.

Brand Deal Tip: Focus on creating content that feels authentic to your followers. If you're promoting a beauty product, showcase it in a natural setting, not a commercial-style pitch. This increases trust and drives higher engagement.

Lesson 3: Using Affiliate Links Effectively

Practical Step 1: Join an Affiliate Program

How to Join:

1. Sign up for affiliate programs such as Amazon Associates, ShareASale, or Rakuten.

2. After approval, find products that align with your niche. For instance, if you're in fitness, join programs like Bodybuilding.com or Fitbit.

Practical Step 2: Use Link in Bio

Set Up: Use a tool like Linktree to add multiple affiliate links in your TikTok bio.

1. Create a Linktree account.

2. Add your affiliate links (for example, products you recommend or your own services).

3. In your TikTok bio, include a call-to-action (CTA) like: "Check out my recommendations" with the Linktree link.

Practical Step 3: Create Engaging Content to Promote Products

Video Ideas:

1. Tutorials: Show how to use the product or how it fits into your daily routine.

2. Unboxing: Do a live unboxing of a product you're promoting.

3. Challenges: Create a challenge around the product. Example: "3 days of using this fitness app – here's my progress!"

Practical Step 4: Track Affiliate Sales

Use affiliate platforms like Amazon or ShareASale to track how many clicks and sales you're generating from your links. Keep an eye on which products perform best and create more content around them.

Lesson 4: Driving Followers to Sales Funnels

Practical Step 1: Create a Simple Sales Funnel

Landing Page Creation:

1. Use Gumroad or ConvertKit to create a simple landing page where you can offer free or paid products (eBooks, courses, etc.).

2. Link this page in your TikTok bio with a clear call-to-action like, "Want more tips? Grab my free guide on __!".

Practical Step 2: Use TikTok to Drive Traffic

Post Ideas:

1. Teasers: Create teaser videos where you give a little snippet of the value they'll get from your freebie or paid offer. Example: "Want to lose 5 pounds in 7 days? Here's a sneak peek of my secret! Link in bio."

2. Promote Time-Sensitive Offers: Use scarcity to drive urgency. "Only 10 spots left for my exclusive workout program. Link in bio to sign up!"

Practical Step 3: Engage Your Followers & Nurture Relationships

Use TikTok to build a community around your brand. Regularly engage with your audience by commenting, responding to questions, and creating content based on feedback from your followers.

Quick Action Plan:

1. Join the TikTok Creator Fund: Aim for 10,000 followers and apply for the Creator Fund.

2. Go Live at least once a week and encourage followers to send you gifts.

3. Join Affiliate Programs: Start promoting products related to your niche using affiliate links in your bio.

4. Create Your Own Sales Funnel: Use Gumroad to create a landing page and start promoting your products through TikTok videos.

5. Engage Consistently: Post at least 3 times a week, respond to comments, and participate in trending challenges to grow your reach.

Next: Module 6 – Instagram Monetization

Time to monetize your Instagram account and dive into sponsored posts, Reels, and affiliate marketing!

Module 6: Instagram Monetization

Instagram offers a variety of tools to make money, but like any platform, success depends on your approach. This module will walk you through concrete steps to leverage Instagram for serious monetization.

Lesson 1: Business vs. Creator Accounts – Which One to Choose?

Instagram offers two main account types for monetization:

1. Creator Account:

Best for: Influencers, public figures, or content creators.

Features: You get detailed insights into your audience, more flexibility in managing content, and options like branded content tags for easier partnerships.

2. Business Account:

Best for: Entrepreneurs or brands selling products or services.

Features: This gives you access to business-specific tools like ads, product tagging, and contact buttons.

Practical Step-by-Step:

How to Switch to a Creator or Business Account:

1. Go to Settings on Instagram.

2. Tap Account > Switch to Professional Account.

3. Choose Creator (if you're a content creator) or Business (if you're selling products or services).

Optimize Your Profile:

Profile Photo: Use a clear, high-quality image that represents you or your brand.

Bio: Your bio should describe what you offer and why people should follow you. Include a clear call-to-action (e.g., "Check out my new ebook – link below!").

Link in Bio: Use tools like Linktree to add multiple links (e.g., product links, affiliate links, blog, or YouTube).

Lesson 2: Sponsored Posts & Story Ads – The Key to Cash Flow

Sponsored posts are one of the top ways to make money on Instagram. Brands are willing to pay influencers to promote their products.

How to Get Sponsored Posts:

1. Focus on Engagement:

Engagement is the key factor brands look at when deciding to work with influencers. Post consistently and interact with your followers.

Practical Tip: Respond to comments, DMs, and engage in relevant conversations. Use Instagram's polls, questions, and quizzes in Stories to increase interaction.

2. Pitch to Brands:

Don't wait for brands to reach out to you. Create a media kit that showcases your audience stats (follower count, engagement rates, demographics) and send it to potential brand partners.

Practical Tip:

Create a professional media kit using a free tool like Canva. Your kit should include:

Your profile and audience details

Examples of past sponsored posts

Rates for sponsored posts

3. Negotiate Paid Posts:

Start with $100-$300 per post depending on your audience size and engagement, but feel free to negotiate higher rates as you grow.

Practical Step-by-Step:

Research brands in your niche (e.g., fitness, fashion, beauty) and follow them.

Slide into their DMs or email their marketing department, pitching your collaboration with a media kit.

Set clear terms: How much will you charge per post? What is the brand's goal?

Lesson 3: Reels Bonus & Affiliate Marketing – Turning Content into Cash

Instagram's Reels Bonus program rewards creators who make high-performing Reels with payouts.

1. How to Qualify for the Reels Bonus Program:

Eligibility: Check if you qualify by going to Instagram Settings > Creator > Bonuses.

Create Engaging Reels:

Choose trending songs or audios that fit your niche.

Keep Reels between 15-30 seconds for better engagement.

Use captions, calls to action (e.g., "Tag a friend" or "Follow for more tips"), and relevant hashtags.

Practical Tip:

Track which type of content performs best on your Reels. Use Instagram's Insights to see which Reels get the most views, shares, and saves. Create more content in the same style.

2. Affiliate Marketing on Instagram:

Affiliate Links: Share products you love with affiliate links in your posts, Stories, or bio. You earn a commission every time someone buys through your link.

Practical Tip:

Amazon Associates or ShareASale are great platforms to get started with affiliate links. Choose products relevant to your audience.

Practical Step-by-Step for Affiliate Marketing:

1. Sign up for an affiliate program (e.g., Amazon Associates).

2. Choose products you genuinely believe in and that match your audience.

3. Use Instagram Stories to showcase these products and add affiliate links using the swipe-up feature (or Link Sticker in Stories).

4. In your post captions, include a call-to-action like: "Click the link in my bio to shop this amazing product!"

Lesson 4: Leveraging Bio Links & Product Pages – Drive Conversions

Your bio is valuable space. Use it wisely to drive traffic to your monetization channels, whether that's affiliate links, your online store, or other sales funnels.

1. Use Bio Link Tools: Tools like Linktree or Beacons allow you to add multiple links in your bio, giving you more opportunities to drive traffic.

Practical Tip:

Set up a Linktree (or a similar tool) to organize your links. Include links to affiliate products, blog posts, or a landing page for your services.

2. Instagram Shop – Sell Directly from Instagram:

If you sell products, Instagram Shop lets you tag products directly in your posts and stories. Customers can purchase without leaving the app.

Practical Step-by-Step:

1. Set up your Instagram shop by linking to a Facebook catalog.

2. Tag products in your posts by selecting the Tag Products option when creating a post.

3. Create a Story with product tags for quick access.

Practical Tip:

Post about new arrivals or sales regularly. Use features like countdown stickers or polls in Stories to create excitement around your products.

Practical Implementation Checklist for Instagram Monetization:

1. Switch to a Business or Creator Account to unlock monetization tools.

2. Optimize Your Profile with a strong bio and call-to-action (CTA).

3. Build Engagement: Consistently post content that aligns with your niche and engage with your followers.

4. Pitch Brands for Sponsored Posts: Reach out with a media kit and negotiate payment.

5. Set Up Reels and Affiliate Marketing: Use Reels to build engagement and earn from affiliate links in posts and stories.

6. Leverage Bio Links: Use Linktree or Beacons to link to all your monetization sources.

Conclusion for Instagram Monetization:

Monetizing Instagram requires consistency and strategic planning. By optimizing your profile, creating engaging content, and using the platform's monetization features like affiliate marketing, Reels Bonus, and sponsored posts, you can turn your Instagram account into a profitable business.

Module 7: Monetization Tools & Platforms

In this module, we dive into the tools and platforms that will streamline your monetization process. These are the essential tools every content creator should have in their toolkit to maximize income potential and make the process easier and more efficient. From selling digital products to managing emails and automating your tasks, this section covers it all.

Must-Have Tools: Linktree, Gumroad, Ko-fi, Canva, ConvertKit

1. Linktree: Your All-in-One Link Hub

Linktree is a must-have for any social media creator. It allows you to put all of your important links (like your website, social media profiles, products, and affiliate links) in one place and share it with your audience easily. This tool is perfect for Instagram, TikTok, and even Twitter (X), where you can only include one link in your bio.

Practical Steps:

1. Create a free Linktree account and start adding your most important links.

2. Customize your Linktree landing page to reflect your branding and make it visually appealing.

3. Share your Linktree link in your social media bios.

Pro Tip: Don't just include links to your website or products—use Linktree to promote blog posts, affiliate offers, and even limited-time deals.

2. Gumroad: Selling Digital Products with Ease

Gumroad is a platform that lets you easily sell digital products like ebooks, templates, courses, and art. It's an excellent tool for creators who have content they want to sell but don't have the technical expertise to set up an e-commerce site.

Practical Steps:

1. Sign up for Gumroad and upload your digital products (ebooks, printables, templates, etc.).

2. Set a price for your products, or use Gumroad's Pay What You Want model for flexibility.

3. Promote your products on social media with a call to action to purchase from your Gumroad link.

Pro Tip: Create digital bundles (e.g., "Buy 3 eBooks for $19") to encourage larger purchases from your followers.

3. Ko-fi: Monetizing through Donations and Memberships

Ko-fi allows your followers to support you directly through donations, as well as purchase content and become paying members. This platform works well for creators who produce content regularly but don't want to rely on ad revenue alone.

Practical Steps:

1. Create a Ko-fi page and link it to your social media bios.

2. Offer content on a "pay what you want" basis or provide memberships for exclusive access to your work.

3. Use Ko-fi's Shop feature to sell your digital products directly to your audience.

Pro Tip: Offer exclusive content for members who pledge a certain amount per month. For example, provide behind-the-scenes content or early access to your new projects.

4. Canva: Design with Ease

Canva is an all-in-one design tool that allows creators to easily create eye-catching graphics for social media posts, presentations, posters, and more. With Canva's templates and drag-and-drop functionality, you can create professional-looking designs without needing graphic design skills.

Practical Steps:

1. Sign up for a free Canva account (or the Pro version for even more features).

2. Use Canva's templates to create engaging social media graphics—Instagram posts, Stories, YouTube thumbnails, Pinterest pins, etc.

3. Use Canva Pro features like brand kits to keep your branding consistent across platforms.

Pro Tip: Create multiple versions of the same content for different platforms (e.g., Instagram post vs. Instagram Story) to maximize engagement without extra effort.

5. ConvertKit: Building and Nurturing an Email List

Email marketing is one of the most effective ways to generate consistent income. ConvertKit is a powerful email marketing platform that allows you to build an email list, create automated email sequences, and manage campaigns easily. It's especially helpful for creators selling products, services, or subscriptions.

Practical Steps:

1. Sign up for ConvertKit and integrate it with your website or social media.

2. Create email opt-ins to start building your email list (e.g., free resources like an ebook or exclusive tips).

3. Set up automated email sequences to nurture your subscribers and encourage them to purchase your products or services.

Pro Tip: Offer exclusive discounts or bonuses to subscribers who join your email list, giving them extra value while boosting your revenue.

Creating and Selling Digital Products

Creating digital products is one of the most scalable ways to monetize your audience. Products like ebooks, online courses, printables, and digital art require upfront effort but can generate passive income once created.

Types of Digital Products to Sell:

1. Ebooks: Share your expertise or stories with your audience. Platforms like Amazon Kindle Direct Publishing (KDP) make it easy to self-publish and sell ebooks.

2. Online Courses: Teach your skills or knowledge with video-based courses. Platforms like Teachable or Thinkific provide an easy way to create and sell courses.

3. Printables: Sell things like planners, journals, or design templates. Websites like Etsy or Gumroad make it easy to sell digital files.

4. Stock Photos & Graphics: If you're a photographer or designer, selling stock images and graphics on sites like Shutterstock or Adobe Stock can be a lucrative revenue stream.

Practical Steps to Create Digital Products:

1. Choose your product (ebook, course, printable, etc.).

2. Create high-quality content—use your expertise or hire a professional if necessary.

3. Set up an online store (using Gumroad or Etsy) to sell your digital product.

4. Promote your digital product on your social media channels.

Using Email Lists for Passive Income

Building an email list isn't just about sending out newsletters—it's about creating a pipeline to generate income. Once you have a list of engaged subscribers, you can promote products, courses, and affiliate offers directly to them.

How to Monetize Your Email List:

1. Affiliate Marketing: Send tailored offers for products or services that align with your audience's interests.

2. Product Launches: When you create your own products (ebooks, courses, etc.), use your email list to promote them to your most engaged followers.

3. Memberships or Subscriptions: Offer exclusive content or community access in exchange for a monthly fee.

4. Sponsored Emails: If you have a large enough list, companies might pay to have their products featured in your email newsletter.

Practical Steps:

1. Create a lead magnet (something valuable that people will give their email address for, such as an ebook, checklist, or course preview).

2. Set up automated email sequences to nurture your list and drive sales.

3. Promote your products or affiliate products directly to your email subscribers.

Final Thought: Putting It All Together

Now that you know the essential tools for monetization and how to create your digital products, the next step is consistency. Use these platforms and tools to streamline your content creation, connect with your audience, and turn your social media presence into a profit-generating machine.

By combining the power of these tools with your content strategy, you'll have everything you need to start earning consistently from your social media platforms.

Module 8: Scaling and Automation

"Don't work harder, work smarter—then let systems work for you."

By this stage, you've built your online presence and started making money. Now it's time to scale your efforts without burning out by using automation, repurposing, and smart outsourcing.

1. Repurposing Content Across Platforms

Think of your content like pizza dough—you can slice it into many formats and serve it in different styles. Here's how to do it effectively:

Example:

You create a 5-minute YouTube video titled: **"5 Habits of Successful Creators."**

Instagram Reel: Take a 30-second clip where you talk about Habit #3. Add captions using CapCut.

Twitter Thread: Break down each habit into a tweet. Add a CTA linking to the full video.

Pinterest Pin: Turn the key takeaways into an infographic using Canva.

Facebook Post: Share a behind-the-scenes photo from filming + a quote from the video.

Action Step:

1. Pick ONE piece of content (video, blog, or tweet)

2. List 3 different platforms you can reuse it on

3. Use Canva, CapCut, or ChatGPT to help transform it

Pro Tools:

CapCut (editing short videos for Reels/TikToks)

Lumen5 (turn blogs into videos)

Canva (resize graphics for all platforms)

2. Scheduling & Automating Like a Pro

Posting manually every day = burn out. You need a system.

Practical Workflow:

Monday: Plan your weekly posts (educational, story, promo)

Tuesday: Batch create content

Wednesday: Schedule them using a tool

Example Schedule:

Monday: Instagram Story (Poll)

Tuesday: Facebook post (share a tip)

Wednesday: Tweet (relatable insight)

Thursday: Instagram Reel (funny but helpful)

Friday: Email newsletter with weekly recap

Top Scheduling Tools:

Buffer / Later: Schedule IG, Facebook, Twitter, Pinterest

Metricool: Great for analytics + scheduling

Notion / Trello: Plan your content calendar

3. Automating Sales Funnels

If you're selling anything—ebooks, services, coaching—build a simple funnel:

Example Funnel:

1. Instagram Bio Link → Free checklist ("10 Tools I Use to Make Money Online")

2. User signs up → Email welcome sequence with value-packed tips

3. Day 3 email → Offer your $9.99 ebook or service

Tools to Use:

ConvertKit: Automate email sequences

Gumroad / Payhip: Sell digital products

Zapier: Automate actions (e.g., auto-tag a customer when they buy)

4. Outsourcing and Building a Team

You don't need to do it all. Here's what to hand off:

What to Outsource First:

Video editing (Fiverr / Upwork)

Caption writing (AI or freelancers)

Customer DMs (VA or chatbot)

Example:

You spend 4 hours a week editing Reels.

Hire a Fiverr editor for $10/video → You save 4 hours, which you can use to create more content or pitch brands.

Tip:

Create a Google Doc with your style guide (font, colors, tone) to make onboarding fast.

Tools to manage your team:

Notion – Assign tasks + organize SOPs

Slack – Communicate with team

Loom – Record explainer videos for your VAs

5. Scaling What Works

Let the data tell you where to double down.

Example:

You noticed your TikTok about "How I made my first $100 online" got 50K views.

Repurpose that into:

A blog post

A YouTube Short

A lead magnet ("My $100 Monetization Blueprint")

An email sequence with affiliate links

Track these metrics weekly:

Best performing post per platform

Most clicked link

Highest converting funnel

Use:

Google Analytics

Instagram Insights

YouTube Studio

Bitly to track clicks

Mini Challenge: 7-Day Scaling Plan

Day 1: Identify 1 high-performing post

Day 2: Repurpose it to 2 other formats

Day 3: Batch-schedule 5 days of content

Day 4: Set up your freebie + email funnel

Day 5: Delegate one task to a freelancer

Day 6: Review your analytics

Day 7: Double down on what worked best

Final Thought:

Scaling doesn't mean doing more. It means doing less, better—with systems. When you repurpose smartly, automate wisely, and delegate effectively, you free up energy to innovate and grow.

Next Up: Module 9 – The Pitfalls to Avoid (so you don't lose everything you built).

Module 9: Mistakes That Kill Monetization

"It's not just what you do—it's what you avoid that saves your income."

Let's be real: one wrong move on social media can ruin your progress. Whether it's an overlooked platform policy, fake followers, or messy branding—these are the silent killers of your growth and monetization.

This module is about recognizing those traps and avoiding them like a pro.

1. Platform Violations & Shadowbans

You could be creating killer content, but if the algorithm flags you—you're done.

Real-World Example:

A TikTok creator was earning via brand deals. They used copyrighted music in one viral video. TikTok muted it, restricted their reach, and their next 10 videos flopped. Brands backed out.

Avoid This:

Read the platform's monetization policies. (Every platform has them!)

Don't use copyrighted music or stolen content.

Avoid excessive hashtags, clickbait titles, or misleading thumbnails.

Pro Tip:

Use royalty-free music from platforms like Epidemic Sound or YouTube's Audio Library.

2. Inconsistent Branding & Content Confusion

When your audience doesn't "get" what you're about, they won't follow—or buy.

Example:

Your Instagram bio says "Fitness Tips," but your last 5 posts are memes, selfies, and random tweets. Result? Confused followers and no growth.

Fix It Fast:

Choose a clear content lane (e.g., "budget travel," "productivity hacks," "Christian motivation")

Keep a consistent visual style (colors, fonts, editing)

Reinforce your niche in your bio and profile banners

Quick Exercise:

Google your name or handle. Do the search results, bio, and content align with what you want to be known for? If not—edit everything until they do.

3. Fake Followers, Bots & Engagement Tricks

Yes, that "Get 10K followers in 24 hours" DM is a scam.

What Happens When You Buy Followers:

Your engagement rate tanks

You can't get brand deals

Platforms may suspend or demonetize your account

Instead, Do This:

Use engagement pods only with real people, not bots

Focus on niche content + hashtags to grow organically

Collaborate with others in your space (Lives, shoutouts, interviews)

4. Over-Monetizing Too Early

Don't push products or ask for money when you haven't built trust yet.

Example:

You have 300 followers and you're already asking people to "Subscribe to my Patreon." Slow down. Focus on giving value first.

Do This Instead:

Provide free value for your first 30-60 days

Offer free lead magnets like checklists or guides

Build your email list before launching paid offers

5. Ignoring Analytics & Feedback

You're not guessing anymore. You're running a business. And data is your best friend.

Example:

You keep posting 60-second reels, but your analytics show your 15-second tips perform better. Why ignore that?

Action Step:

Every week, review:

Top 3 posts by engagement

Best performing CTA

Follower growth and source

Use tools like:

Instagram Insights

YouTube Studio

Twitter/X Analytics

Google Analytics (for your funnel or website)

Mini Checklist: Avoid These Mistakes

Read the monetization rules of each platform

Keep branding consistent everywhere

Never buy followers—ever

Don't sell before you serve

Track what's working and improve it weekly

Final Thought:

Success isn't just about creating great content—it's about creating smart, safe, and strategic content. Protect your income by avoiding these traps, and your growth will feel like it's on autopilot.

Coming Up: Module 10 – Your 30-Day Monetization Action Plan

(Where we bring all the pieces together and turn your knowledge into income)

Module 10: 30-Day Monetization Action Plan

"Execute like your income depends on it—because it does."

This is where your knowledge turns into actual income. You've learned the mindset, the platforms, the tools, and the mistakes to avoid. Now, it's time to apply.

Each week in this 30-day plan is laser-focused on moving you closer to monetization. No fluff. Just action.

Week 1: Setup & Strategy

Goal: Lay the foundation for profitable content and clear branding.

Action Steps:

Choose your primary platform (start with ONE)

Create or optimize your profile:

Bio = Who you help + How you help + CTA

Example: "Helping moms make money from home | Free guide in bio"

Switch to Creator/Business account (if applicable)

Pick your niche & target audience (be specific)

Write your brand pillars (3 topics you'll talk about consistently)

Deliverables by end of week:

Optimized profile + link in bio (use Linktree, Ko-fi, or Beacons)

Clear brand voice and visuals (Canva templates help!)

First 7 content ideas brainstormed

Week 2: Content & Engagement

Goal: Start building trust and growing organically.

Action Steps:

Post 3–5 times this week (content = value + story + CTA)

Use proper hashtags (mix large, medium & niche tags)

Go live or post a story each day

Engage with 10 accounts per day in your niche (comment meaningfully)

Reply to all DMs and comments (build community)

Content Ideas:

"My story" post – how you got into your niche

A quick how-to or tip carousel

Behind-the-scenes or workday vlog

Problem-solution reel (e.g., "Struggling to grow? Try this...")

Deliverables by end of week:

3–5 quality posts live

20–30 new engaged followers

1 mini-viral or "save-worthy" post

Week 3: Monetize & Promote

Goal: Introduce a product, service, or affiliate offer.

Action Steps:

Create a freebie or low-ticket offer ($5–$20) Examples:

A digital planner on Gumroad

A mini eBook on Canva

A "Top 10 Tips" checklist with affiliate links

Add it to your link-in-bio

Announce it with urgency:

"Launching this guide for the first 50 people!"

Use email marketing or DMs to offer it to your followers

Affiliate Example:

Join Amazon Associates or ClickBank. Create a post:

"Here's the mic I use for all my content. Game-changer! [Affiliate link]"

Deliverables by end of week:

1 product or affiliate offer launched

At least 1 sale or 5 new email subscribers

Testimonials or screenshots saved for credibility

Week 4: Evaluate & Scale

Goal: Double down on what works. Cut what doesn't. Plan for growth.

Action Steps:

Analyze best-performing content (likes, shares, saves, click-throughs)

Survey your audience: "What do you want more of?"

Repurpose your top 3 posts (turn a reel into a carousel, etc.)

Batch-create next week's content using templates

Consider cross-posting to a second platform

Bonus Tasks:

Explore scheduling tools (e.g., Buffer, Later, Metricool)

Identify 2 influencers in your niche to collaborate with

Start building an email list with a ConvertKit free plan

Deliverables by end of week:

Content plan for next month

Clear strategy for your next offer

A growing brand with real momentum

30-Day Summary Checklist

Optimized profile & branding

Consistent value-driven content

Community engagement & follower growth

One offer launched (product, service, or affiliate)

Audience feedback + analytics reviewed

A rinse-and-repeat system in place

Final Thoughts:

You've just completed your first real monetization sprint. Most people consume courses and never apply them. You're different—you took action. Keep going.

Because the truth is:

Monetization isn't a one-time event. It's a lifestyle.

Stay visible. Stay valuable. Stay authentic.

Your digital empire has just begun.

Conclusion: From Passion to Profit – The Journey Begins Now

You've made it to the end of Social Media Monetization Mastery: A Complete Course to Turn Your Platforms into Profit—but really, this is just the beginning.

You've learned how to shift your mindset from consumer to creator. You've studied how to earn on Facebook, Twitter, YouTube, TikTok, and Instagram. You now understand how to turn your passion into income using tools, strategy, and consistency.

But reading this book won't make you money.

Action will.

Success doesn't come to those who merely scroll and consume—it comes to those who apply, create, fail forward, and stay consistent. You don't need a million followers. You just need to start showing up with value, solving problems, and telling your story.

Remember this:

People pay attention to authenticity.

Brands pay for influence.

Audiences pay for solutions.

And the internet rewards momentum.

So, start messy if you must. Launch with what you have. Tweak, test, grow—and monetize as you go.

The digital world has leveled the playing field. It doesn't matter who you are or where you're starting from. What matters is what you do next.

Now go build your digital empire.

I'll be watching from the sidelines, cheering you on.